JOBS
TO BE
PROUD OF

Profiles of Workers Who Are Blind or Visually Impaired

Deborah Kendrick
Preface by Linda Ellerbee

PRESS
New York

97   96   95   94   93   5   4   3   2   1

Printed in the United States of America

Library of Congress Cataloging-in-Publication Data

Kendrick, Deborah, 1950-
     Jobs to be proud of : profiles of workers who are blind
 or visually impaired / Deborah Kendrick.
          p.   cm.
     ISBN 0-89128-258-0
          1. Blind—Employment—United States—Case studies. 2.
 Visually handicapped—Employment—United States—Case studies.   I.
 Title.
     HV1655.K46   1993   93-27408
     331.5'91—dc20   CIP

Contents

Foreword

SATISFYING WORK is part of a full and productive life for most adults, but nowadays it often seems as though meaningful jobs are particularly hard to find. This may be especially true for people who are blind or visually impaired, who have higher unemployment rates than do people who are sighted. But the 12 people you will read about in *Jobs To Be Proud Of: Profiles of Workers Who Are Blind or Visually Impaired* not only have jobs, they have jobs that they enjoy and in which they thrive.

The stories of these 12 job holders contain valuable lessons for us. They reflect the diversity of the kinds of work that people who are blind or visually impaired perform and that can be done without an advanced academic education or extensive technological adaptations. They show the ways in which a vital and engaging group of people followed their own interests and preferences to obtain jobs that are meaningful to them. And they reveal the perceptions of blind and visually impaired people themselves because all those profiled in this book share their insights with us and because the writer who interviewed them is herself blind.

We at the American Foundation for the Blind believe that *Jobs To Be Proud Of* will be a particularly valuable resource for blind adults and adolescents

and their families, educators, rehabilitation counselors, and employers. We hope that the experiences
described in this book offer insights and creative
approaches to employment for people with visual
impairments. And we thank the individuals who
agreed to be interviewed for this book, who provided photographs for it, and who consented to allow
us to get to know them and their work.

Carl R. Augusto
President and Executive Director
American Foundation for the Blind

Preface

WHEN DEBORAH KENDRICK was growing up, "experts" told her she couldn't be a writer. It was unrealistic, they said, because she was both blind and a woman. Today Deborah Kendrick is still blind, still a woman—and one helluva writer. The thing is, she seems to see the world more clearly than those of us who only see with our eyes.

I read her newspaper columns in the *Cincinnati Enquirer* every chance I get. Deborah Kendrick writes clearly and eloquently on a subject I know far too little about: what it's like to live with a disability. The lesson I take away from this book—from all her writing—is that the disability is usually mine. In other words, I need to rethink how I look at someone who's blind or in a wheelchair. I need to learn something new. In that, I am not unlike most people, I suspect, which is why I'm glad Deborah Kendrick is out there to remind us of what we need to know.

If we are to create a world that is a friendly place to people who have all different kinds of abilities, a world that is safe and accessible to all, then we need better guides. I like to think Deborah Kendrick is one of the best.

Linda Ellerbee
Award-winning author
and television journalist

Introduction

THIS BOOK contains a dozen love stories. They are stories of people who love their work, love life, and love themselves enough to believe that they can, with the proper mix of opportunity and ingenuity, go wherever their interests and aptitudes take them. They are also love stories from the perspective that I, in my attempt to understand these people and the jobs they do, fell in love with each and every one of them.

Each of the people in this book happens to be blind or visually impaired, and each is doing a job that does not require a college education. It was not difficult to find them. The only hardship, in fact, was in restricting the focus to only 12 people and 12 jobs. In the end, my only rule for inclusion was diversity—a diversity of age, gender, race, geographic region, visual acuity, type of job, and level of education. The employers are diverse, too. Some of the people profiled here are employed by government agencies, some by private businesses, and some by long-standing programs within the blindness system. Others are self-employed. It seemed particularly important to include individuals employed in the blindness system—individuals who have found employment within the National Industries for the Blind's network of workshops and the Randolph-

Sheppard Vending Program—because this is a book about real work for real money, and both of these programs are putting thousands of real people to work.

A number of sometimes disturbing refrains were sung by the people in this book as I listened to their stories, and one of them was the recurring theme of prejudice. There is prejudice on the job, certainly, and among the uninitiated sighted public. Even more distressing, however, are the prejudices among people who are themselves blind or who are professionals helping blind people. Pat Votta, a piano tuner and technician, commented that, had he known the rank of inferiority blind people have assigned to his profession, he might never have gotten into it. Similarly, Ardis Bazyn cited as one of the few serious disadvantages of her job as a participant in the Business Enterprise Program that other blind people sometimes think her job is "nothing."

Many professionals in the blindness field also have a tendency to make assumptions about the capabilities and work of others. When I was 16, I encountered my first vocational rehabilitation counselor. He was a nice man, a blind man, in fact, and he was going to help send me to college.

There was no doubt that I could and should go to college: My ability to perform in the academic arena had been demonstrated. What I could not do, my counselor told me, was be a writer. His conclusion was based on experience: He was not a writer; he had never had a client who was a writer; he knew no blind person working as a writer. No matter what our intentions, it seems we are all subject to the error of resisting the unknown.

"They wanted to send me to college because they don't think a blind person can do anything else," quipped Gary Petsch, a talented mechanic who is blind, in reference to another stereotype held by vocational rehabilitation counselors today. This leaning toward academics is an ironic twist, indeed, on our employment position as blind people in history. In our enlightened 20th-century wisdom, we congratulate ourselves for no longer expecting blind people to weave baskets or make brooms; instead, we want all of them to earn advanced degrees in law or computer science. Yet each of the people in these pages sings the refrain of pride in work well done and in a strong sense of personal achievement. Some went to college; most did not. All are doing jobs that could be a blind person's sole support. And there are other common threads tying them together as well. Many seem to work harder and have more education than their sighted peers. Some have had to fight tenaciously, even to the point of taking unwanted college courses in another field, to be given a chance to exercise innate abilities in a work environment, and nearly all emphasized that acceptance of blindness, albeit high, came only after a period of proving themselves as people of ability and as equals.

The jobs held by the people in this book are not necessarily the 12 best or most appropriate ones for blind people who want work not requiring a college degree. Nor are the job-specific accommodations to visual impairment the only ones possible. The salaries, benefits, and work circumstances shown are individual, as jobs, abilities, and people tend to be, and may vary in different situations and parts of the country. They are simply a starting place, a spark for the imagination, and an inkling of the possibilities that exist.

This book is for anyone who is blind or visually impaired and who wants to work. It is for the families and friends of people who are blind or visually impaired. It is for every guidance counselor, vocational rehabilitation counselor, and job placement professional who might ever be in a position to help a blind person choose a career. And it is for anyone who has any doubts about the abilities of someone who cannot see.

—D.K.

Jobs To Be Proud Of

CHILD CARE PROVIDER
LaSandra Stewart

"I just loved taking care of children."

HOME
Barberton, Ohio

EMPLOYER
Self-employed

AGE
31

CAUSE OF VISUAL IMPAIRMENT
Congenital glaucoma

VISUAL ACUITY
20/200 in one eye, no vision in the other

THERE IS a certain serenity about LaSandra Stewart that makes it clear why children adore her. She is calm, patient, loves beautiful things in art and nature, and enjoys sharing that appreciation with children. She is no great fan of television, she says, so finding interesting activities for children when she is in charge is, for her, a natural response.

Stewart began her child care career working as the full-time caregiver for the Carrachers, an Akron, Ohio, family with two young daughters. When their younger child was eight weeks old,

Stewart was hired. She came to the house every weekday for the next six years.

Although she is a natural for the job, Stewart had not always planned to work as a child care provider. After her 1980 graduation from Firestone High School in Akron, Stewart took classes at the University of Akron on and off through 1986. Her glaucoma was causing headaches, and the extensive reading was exhausting. Finally, her doctor recommended that she try something else.

"I had done a lot of baby-sitting for friends," Stewart recalls. "Not for money. I just loved taking care of children." Happily for her, she was able to turn something she loved doing into a source of needed income. She responded to an ad the Carrachers placed and landed a satisfying job and a family of friends in the bargain.

Stewart is not the only person satisfied with the work she does; her employer is full of praise for her. "She is just excellent," raves Dennis Carracher. "For one thing, she was here every morning regularly, without fail, and the kids are crazy about her. She didn't just let them sit around and watch TV. She always had all kinds of projects for them to do, and we're really hoping to get her back for summers."

For Stewart's part, she says with some modesty that the projects were just doing what came naturally. Because she prefers the safety of familiar environments when responsible for young children, she says outings were just walks around the immediate neighborhood.

"Elizabeth was naturally interested in trees," Stewart cites as an example, "so we'd look at acorns. We'd collect a bag of them—and then come home and make interesting things with our collection." Her own penchant for creativity—calligraphy, needlework, drawing, and painting—benefits the children she cares for, both on the job and as a teacher of preschoolers in Sunday school.

Diapering, feeding, and tending babies and toddlers are all pleasures, Stewart says, that present her little difficulty. "I did wish at times," she recalls, "that the Carrachers had a thermometer I could read when Elizabeth was a baby," but she honed her guesses to be reasonably accurate.

Although she reads large print, Stewart often uses hand magnifiers to manage it. Even with magnifiers she has difficulty reading some children's books, which can have peculiar layouts. "There was one favorite book of Elizabeth's," she says, "that had the words interwoven throughout beautiful illustrations. For me, the print was hard to find."

However, in Stewart's experience, children love to help in little ways. They understand, for example, when she tells them that it is necessary for her to take time first to read a page and then to enjoy the illustrations. Sharing a book with a child, she says, is probably a longer process for her than it is for most people, but children do not mind at all.

For mobility, Stewart sometimes uses a white cane, although mostly for identification purposes. She believes that the cane provides added safety for both herself and the child when she is responsible for a small child while walking and that it makes clear to others that she is visually impaired.

Having someone capable in charge of their children is more important to most parents than are logistics such as the ability to drive. Although Stewart traveled to and from the Carrachers' home via paratransit (public transportation for people with disabilities) most days, there were times when Dennis Carracher had to pick her up. Similarly, if either of the girls had a doctor's or dentist's appointment, the Carrachers handled transportation arrangements. Dennis Carracher barely seemed to notice.

The Carracher children, now 6 and 13, are both in all-day school and need an adult caregiver only in the summer. For Stewart, however, work continues. Almost immediately, friends saw an opportunity and hired her to care for their 3- and 4-year-old daughters. Again, the work is full time.

Paying attention to safety issues is probably the only adaptation Stewart believes she has made as a person who is visually impaired. "It is important always to make sure that all small objects are picked up from the floor with babies and toddlers," she says, "and to cook without the children in the kitchen." She has no doubt that the children understand her vision problem. "They like to explain to other people when I have difficulty with something," she laughs, "that I just 'can't see very good.'"

A close relationship with the Carracher children continues (now that 6-year-old-Elizabeth uses the telephone, she calls Stewart frequently to tell her about school, and both children send drawings and notes), and Stewart is rapidly growing attached to two more little girls. She may not be caring for other people's children forever, she says, with her characteristic peacefulness, "but it is very definitely rewarding work."

PAY AND BENEFITS: In self-employment, Stewart earns $4–5 per hour, or up to $100 per week. Child care providers in other parts of the United States can earn up to $250 per week. In Stewart's case, health care is available through Medicaid. Vacation time is a trade-off: Stewart can notify families when she will be taking off, but a vacation for anyone in self-employment means time without pay, unless an agreement regarding paid vacation is reached.

CUSTOMER SERVICE AGENT
Scott Hooker

"A person with a visual impairment not only can do the same job as a sighted worker but can do it well."

HOME
Decatur, Georgia

EMPLOYER
Federal Express Corporation

AGE
38

CAUSE OF BLINDNESS
Retinopathy of prematurity

VISUAL ACUITY
No vision

FIVE YEARS ago, Scott Hooker needed a job and believes he was "in the right place at the right time." After his 1976 graduation from Berry College, he held a series of part-time or short-term jobs, ranging from Dictaphone typing to playing piano in Atlanta nightclubs. The prospect of getting married, however, emphasized his need for reliable regular income, and he sought solutions from his state vocational rehabilitation counselor.

As it happened, Federal Express had been exploring the possibility of hiring someone with a visual impairment to work as a customer service agent. After a computer evaluation at the Atlanta Rehabilitation Center, Hooker proved himself to be a prime candidate.

Although all other customer service agents work at dumb terminals, Hooker's workstation consists of a computer (a 286 machine with terminal emulation hardware, a screen-access program, and a speech synthesizer). A full computer was necessary for Hooker to run JAWS (Job Access with Speech), the screen- access program he uses to access the information relevant to his job. A headset was also customized, which enables him to be tuned into a telephone line with one ear while hearing the computer's speech synthesizer with the other. This adaptation, together with the screen-access program's capacity for defining speech windows to monitor several screen areas simultaneously, gives Hooker the tools needed to perform his fast-paced job on a par with his sighted co-workers.

Handling roughly 150 to 170 calls daily, Hooker admits that his job can be stressful. Agents are expected to spend not more than two minutes per phone call and not more than 21 seconds working at the computer between calls.

The substance of those calls runs the gamut from pick-up orders, complaints, and compliments to requests to track packages. If a customer calls to check the status of an order picked up in San Antonio yesterday, for example, Hooker can determine what time it will arrive in St. Louis today.

Hooker's workstation, like those of the other 15 to 20 workers surrounding him during an eight-hour shift, is basically a partitioned cubicle, with a computer and phone console. Although having to listen to a phone conversation with one ear and to a speech synthesizer with the other may appear to be disconcerting, Hooker has adjusted quickly. In his five years on the job, all of his performance reviews have been favorable, and he has been granted every raise and bonus available.

Beyond the computer adaptations for accessing the system, Hooker says there were no other accommodations necessary for him as someone who is blind. For transportation to and from work he uses MARTA, Atlanta's public transportation system of buses and trains. For him, depending on friends was the least reliable method of traveling to work on time.

"The company is excellent about providing feedback," Hooker says, praising in particular the personalized method used to monitor an agent's phone manner. "A manager will sometimes sit with you," he says, "and then comment on strengths and weaknesses." Hooker's ratings are generally high on such job criteria as voice quality, ability to find facts, and overall empathy and interest in what a customer has to say. Because of the need to access the relevant information through speech, he believes that efficiency for a blind person is slightly diminished but predicts that even that should level out as technology advances. One minor detail of the job, for instance, which has been inaccessible to him, is the occasional need to look up zip codes in a print directory. "Now," he points out, "that could be done by a blind person with the installation of a CD-ROM drive and CD-ROM zip code directory."

When Federal Express hired Hooker, it was something of an experiment. After five years, that experiment has had tremendous payoffs—for the company, for Scott Hooker, and for some other people who are blind. Hooker was recently promoted to the position of senior information planning analyst, and his new role will be to help identify, accommodate, and train 50 new customer service representatives who are blind and will work at the company's locations around the country. Clearly, experience has been the best teacher in communicating Scott Hooker's message that "a person with a visual impairment not only can do the same job as a sighted worker but can do it well."

PAY AND BENEFITS: $7.61 per hour to begin; up to $12.65, with possible biannual raises and bonuses. Good medical coverage, with the option to buy family coverage. Two weeks of vacation time are earned after one year, three weeks after five years, and four weeks after ten years.

FACTORY WORKER
Todd Barnum

"People need to see that a blind person can work in the real world, doing a real job."

HOME
Colorado Springs, Colorado

EMPLOYER
Schlage Lock Company

AGE
32

CAUSE OF BLINDNESS
German measles during mother's pregnancy

VISUAL ACUITY
Legally blind since birth; sees shapes and colors but cannot use print

"PART OF what makes me so doggone happy about my job," says Todd Barnum, "is that it's just an ordinary job. So many institutions and agencies advise people who are blind to become rehab counselors or fit somewhere else back in the blindness system. People need to see that a blind person can work in the real world, doing a real job, and doing 95 percent of the same work everyone else is doing there."

Barnum's "real job" involves assembling various types of locks as an assembly worker at Schlage Lock Company, a Colorado Springs manufacturing plant employing over 1,000 workers. For Todd Barnum, working on the line at Schlage began four and a half years ago, after a long, discouraging search for work.

Born in Salt Lake City, Utah, Barnum had an eye condition that was diagnosed at birth as being a result of his mother's bout with German measles during pregnancy. Legally blind is his definition for his visual impairment—although his minimal sight includes only shapes and colors—and he has been grateful for braille since his early days as a student at first the Utah State School and later the Colorado State School for the Deaf and Blind. Barnum attended public high school in Colorado Springs and then spent five years attending a community college, earning a two-year degree in precision machining. He does not regret the effort but says he himself soon decided that "the machine shop world was not yet ready for a blind person."

Barnum entered a job training program at Goodwill Industries, a place where he had been temporarily employed after high school graduation, and was assigned to an assembly project that led to his being hired by Schlage. "Goodwill had a contract with Schlage," he recalls, "and I worked for about a month on that contract. The people at Goodwill helped me get the first interview with Schlage, and the fact that I was already doing similar work probably helped me get the job."

His first eight months were on the night shift, working 4:30 P.M. to 12:30 A.M., and Barnum did not mind at all. Then and now, his job was essentially the same: assembling by hand or machine various components of levered lock products sold by his employer. Barnum is a member of a nine-person group, and his job varies somewhat from day to day. He describes the hand-building of a six-part lock spring cage as a typical example.

"First," he explains, "you grease a bottom plate. Then you put together a driver, which consists of two C-shaped springs. The driver goes on the bottom plate between two lobes, and you put a lid on the whole thing to hold it together."

Barnum's job then entails his running each spring cage through a crimper, a machine that meshes the metal parts tightly together, and frequently operating other machines as well. "It's all so simple a four-year-old could do it," he laughs, but certainly no four-year-old could build 81 units in an hour or run 411 through the crimper per hour, which is the standard expected of Barnum and all workers in his group.

Learning to do new kinds of assembly is a fairly casual matter for Barnum. Another worker, the immediate supervisor, or the material handler—anyone who already understands how parts must be fit together—will sit with him one-on-one to show him a new operation.

At this point, there is no special equipment for Todd Barnum as a blind person at Schlage, although he hopes that when a planned-for computer is added in subassembly, the company will install it with a speech synthesizer and screen-access program for him. When he was hired, he was provided with taped editions of the employee handbook, and when all workers were required to participate in a YRIQ ("Your Role in Quality") seminar, his employers prepared in advance by having all written materials transcribed into braille.

"If there's a memo going around," he says, "someone will just come by and read it to me, so I know what's going on." The only part of his job, in fact, that Barnum cannot do independently is a small amount of paperwork. Individual efficiency reports are sometimes filled out for him by co-workers, and sometimes he will type an accumulation of his own efficiency records at home and bring them to work. Perhaps his most visible adaptation is Flyer, the yellow Labrador dog guide accompanying him to and from work each day. Because assembly work is mostly sitting or standing in one place, Barnum says he keeps the dog's leash hooked to a belt loop to keep track of him while on the job.

Barnum's days begin at 6:15 A.M., when he and Flyer leave home, and his shift ends at 3:20 each afternoon. "I bought a home about ten blocks from work last year," he explains, "so that I could be solely responsible for getting me to work on time."

His blindness, Barnum says, is accepted by those who work with him and only misconstrued by those who do not. The reality, though, as he puts it, is that "I do a real job in the real world, and it's important for John Q. Public to see that I can do that."

PAY AND BENEFITS: $7.49 per hour, which is the maximum for Barnum's current job. Good medical coverage and retirement plan. Ten days of paid vacation.

FOOD SERVICE MANAGER
Ardis Bazyn

"It feels good to know that you're providing a needed service to people."

HOME
Cedar Rapids, Iowa

EMPLOYER
Self-employed, Business Enterprise Program

AGE
41

CAUSE OF BLINDNESS
Severed optic nerve resulting from auto accident

VISUAL ACUITY
No vision

ARDIS BAZYN had worked as a bookkeeper right after high school graduation, and when she lost her sight at age 20, the idea of going to college to get a job was far from appealing. The Business Enterprise Program, through which people who are blind are trained to operate food service facilities in federally owned buildings, suited her notion of a speedy return to the job market well. It was also a good match for her bookkeeping skills and skills in working with people. After three and a half months in training at the Cleveland Society for the Blind, Bazyn was ready for action.

"Food service is a job that a blind person can handle with confidence," Bazyn says, "provided you get the right training. The Business Enterprise Program offers a wide range of opportunity if you're willing to work and can move to where the locations are available."

In her 20-year career in food service, Bazyn has managed everything from a simple snack bar where she was on her own to a full-blown cafeteria with 13 employees. For the past eight years, she has operated an "all vending" business. Headquartered in the main Cedar Rapids post office, Bazyn's business supplies 30 vending machines, spanning six Cedar Rapids facilities. In her machines, customers can find anything from coffee and soft drinks to candy, snacks, sandwiches, muffins, and yogurt. She has two employees: her husband, David Bazyn, who is also visually impaired, and a part-time driver.

Because Bazyn supplies machines at six locations daily, having a driver to carry supplies is essential. The Bazyns generally take a taxi to work, meet the driver there, and load the car in preparation for the daily route. For Ardis Bazyn, days are usually spent at the main location, while her employees stock, clean, and maintain the machines.

What Bazyn does, in short, is manage the business. Bookkeeping, ordering, accepting deliveries, establishing prices, tracking sales, and answering the phone are the chief ingredients of her workday. She keeps all her own records in braille and, with the assistance of a talking calculator, regularly compiles necessary data to dictate to her volunteer reader, who then copies information onto tax and other forms accordingly. The recent acquisition of a computer, she predicts, will make the record-keeping process even more efficient.

The details of the job are numerous. Besides monitoring inventory and ordering supplies, Bazyn has payroll reports to make, state and federal tax records to complete, and monthly sales tax to compute and pay. Accurately ciphering sales tax might alone boggle a less number-oriented mind. Some machines, for instance, carry a mix of products, some of which are taxable and some not. "Candy isn't taxed," Bazyn says as she ticks off the memorized mental list, "but chips are. All breakfast items are, but coffee, pop, and gum are not."

Bazyn pays social security tax regularly for her two employees and files quarterly estimates for herself. She uses an accountant only once a year to complete the Schedule C tax form for the Internal Revenue

Service, but she generally prefers to do all bookkeeping and accounting herself.

Although machines are stocked daily except Sundays, one advantage of the job, Bazyn says, is flexibility. "Tuesdays and Thursdays we usually work only from about 7 A.M. to noon," she points out, "and if you need to take an hour or two off to go to school for a sick child, you can do that." Taking time off means advance preparation—ordering a week ahead, for example—and hiring someone (usually her part-time employee) to keep the machines filled and running. The major disadvantages of the job are that self-employment means no employee benefits and that hiring and firing are inevitable tasks. "No matter how much you dislike someone or the work they do," she says, "it's always hard to fire people."

As manager of her own business, Bazyn considers it essential to know every operation involved. "Some days I stock and clean machines and carry supplies," she says, "just filling in wherever needed." For the most part, though, her forte is in tracking the numbers connected with the vending operation, and she does that well. Last year, gross sales for her 30 machines amounted to $108,000, and job satisfaction ran high. "It feels good," she says, "to know that you're providing a needed service to people."

PAY AND BENEFITS: Bazyn clears about $22,000 a year, but average earnings in the program vary widely from state to state and among types of vending facilities. Bazyn buys private medical coverage and established her own retirement plan. Manages about four weeks of vacation annually.

IN-FLIGHT PACKAGER
LaWana Miller

"What you make of any job is up to you. But whatever job you do, you should do your best at it."

HOME
Cincinnati, Ohio

EMPLOYER
Cincinnati Association for the Blind, workshop

AGE
59

CAUSE OF BLINDNESS
Unknown, but congenital

VISUAL ACUITY
20/200

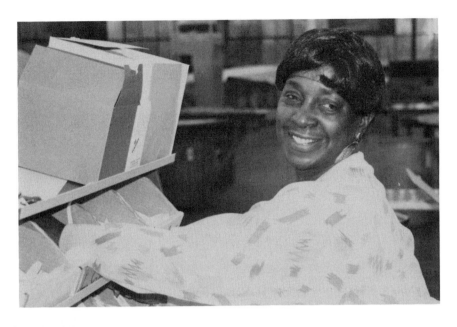

"WHAT YOU MAKE of any job," says LaWana Miller, "is up to you. But whatever job you do, you should do your best at it." That philosophy has accompanied Miller through 32 years of employment at the Cincinnati Association for the Blind, a National Industries for the Blind workshop. Whether packing bars of soap, labeling boxes of detergent, or wrapping packages of Play-Doh, Miller takes pride in the work she does and the connection it gives her to the consumers who will ultimately use the product.

Currently, her job is assembling airline dining packets to be purchased by the U.S. military and used by service personnel in flight. Sitting in her place on the assembly line, Miller selects one item from each of the boxes arranged before her—containing knives, forks, spoons, salt, pepper, sugar, chewing gum, toothpicks, and can openers—places them on a napkin, and slides them into a plastic bag. There are 11 items in all to handle, and the work takes on a certain rhythm of its own.

"The important thing is to be independent," Miller says proudly, knowing as she approaches her 60th birthday that she has succeeded. Although Miller generally falls short of standard quotas for this particular assembly job, she feels good about her work and about understanding her visual impairment.

Managing as a public school student in Middletown, Ohio, was far from easy for Miller 50 years ago. She was a teenager before the reason for her academic struggles was finally recognized as legal blindness. She left school then, in the 11th grade, and worked part time in the kitchen of the Cincinnati Greyhound bus station.

"I had a good time working there," Miller remembers with a chuckle. "They had me washing dishes and making sausages." When she was required to work the cash register, however, being visually impaired made her job difficult. She could not see the numbers on the register, and it seemed time to try another kind of work.

Domestic work and child care were among the earlier ways Miller earned part-time income, but when someone suggested to her that she investigate the possibilities at the Cincinnati Association for the Blind's workshop, she found full-time work that has kept her busy for 32 years. Her first job in the workshop was making products for the military in what was then called the sewing room, and her earnings were $19 a week. Although she says with a grin that "nobody ever makes enough money," Miller concedes that her earnings have multiplied considerably since then.

Each assembly-line job in the workshop carries with it a standard (an expected number of items to be produced per hour) and a piece rate (an amount paid per item). The hourly rate for in-flight dining packets, for example, is $7.43, but if a worker produces above or below the 180-packets-per-hour standard, the pay is adjusted accordingly. "I can afford to live in my own apartment," says Miller to summarize her own situation, "and I go to the national tournament for the American Blind Bowlers Association every year."

Working alongside people of all visual acuities has helped shape Miller's attitude toward people and their abilities. "I've never worked on a job here that didn't have some totally blind people on it, too," she reflects, "and many times they can do things with their hands that I just can't do." She has friends who are totally blind, friends who are visually impaired, and friends who are sighted.

Besides good friends, Miller says her job has given her fair pay and good benefits, such as paid vacation time and medical coverage. It has given her, too, the freedom to commit time to singing in her church choir and continuing her 10-year volunteer commitment to keeping in touch via telephone with a woman unable to leave her home. "Whatever job you do," she advises, "try to keep your independence."

PAY AND BENEFITS: $7.43 per hour, depending on productivity. Agency pays for 60 percent of medical coverage. Vacation after 20 years is four weeks annually.

MASSAGE AND ACUPRESSURE THERAPIST
Susan Kane

"If you are self-motivated, organized, and enjoy providing a sense of physical peace and well-being to others through touch, I would recommend massage therapy as work that can be both psychologically and financially rewarding."

HOME
Burlingame, California

EMPLOYER
Self-employed

AGE
42

CAUSE OF BLINDNESS
Retinopathy of prematurity

VISUAL ACUITY
Usable light perception

SUSAN KANE knew she needed a career change but had no idea what it might be. Her master's degree in music therapy had landed her the directorship of a five-college consortium of Midwest music departments, with an 80-mile radius connecting the five campuses. After six years, Kane was burned out, exhausted, and without a plan. A traffic accident sent her home to northern California for recuperation, and in a part of her treatment that helped her, she found her new direction: acupressure therapy. In 1985, she set up her own acupressure business. In 1986, she added massage therapy to her skills—and the result is a story of job satisfaction and real success.

Massage therapists have found work in the offices of neurosurgeons, chiropractors, physical therapists, sports centers, and elsewhere, but Kane's chosen path has been to establish an office in her home. Upon entering her attractive, well-organized condominium, a new client is escorted down the hall and into the therapy office.

Equipment there is simple: a small desk where Kane takes client histories, a comfortable armchair, a custom-made massage chair, and, of course, at center stage, the massage table itself. Clients come for everything from tennis elbow to emotional stress. They come for relief of aching shoulders after too many hours of desk work or strained lower backs after too much lifting. And they come just because massage is relaxing and therapeutic. Kane's work varies according to each individual's needs, but typically she uses a combination of deep massage and acupressure therapy, in sessions that range from one hour to an hour and a half.

Most business comes by word of mouth and as the result of a twice-annual mailing Kane distributes to a growing mailing list. In that mailing, she offers such customer incentives as discounts for referring friends or relatives, or such options as scheduling one session and getting the second session at a reduced rate.

The training for certification is short but intense. Acupressure therapy and massage therapy require 150 hours of training each for certification in California. (Certification requirements may vary somewhat from state to state.) In Kane's case, courses in both areas (at separate schools) were completed in about nine months altogether. Acupressure, a 5,000-year-old technique of using the fingers to apply prolonged pressure to designated points on the body, is used to relieve stress, headaches, and a host of other maladies. In acupressure training, there are 150 points on the body to learn. "You have to locate them, identify them, and understand their relationship to one another and to the healing process," Kane explains. Since the pace of the training is somewhat individualized, Kane chose to take a given class, take time off at home to write up the accompanying case studies, and then return to school for the next segment. The training itself required no adaptations for Kane's visual impairment, since everyone learned by hands-on recognition of each new set of acupressure points. "The instructor would often demonstrate first on me," Kane recalls, "and then we'd all practice locating points on one another."

In massage therapy training, too, Kane found that the only adaptation she had to make involved determining the best strategies for her for learning. The answer came in three parts: She listened with the rest of her class to the instructor's verbal explanations of massage work, she learned techniques by placing her hands on the hands of others, and she served as the model for class demonstrations.

After becoming certified and establishing a place of business, Kane needed to purchase her table, sheets and pillows, and ordinary office supplies for record keeping. Today, her $45–per–hour charge is essentially profit, with the exception of the ongoing purchase of massage lotion and occasional additions to her collection of soothing music, which accompanies every massage.

The skills necessary to become a massage therapist involve far more than an aptitude for the rote memorization of the names of muscle groups and bones. Beyond reasonable physical strength and a knowledge of basic techniques, one needs to develop the ability to "read" tension through touch and to adjust from a light touch to deep massage from one client to the next.

"Giving a massage is hard work," Kane explains. "I generally can't handle more than four people in a day. The energy doesn't come just from your hands. It's like dancing: It's work that involves your whole body and leaning from the center of your body into the work."

It is important, too, to listen to clients' wishes and remember preferences. Kane relates the example of a client who had been abused in childhood and, as a result, could not tolerate having her feet touched. "It's important to remember and respect that difference," she says.

As someone in business for herself, Kane has

found that marketing and record keeping are also essential elements of her job. She keeps detailed braille accounts of every client and every receipt. One three-ring binder serves as a braille appointment book and another as an account ledger. Clients pay after each session, and Kane's reader assists with mailing receipts once a week. The only "technology" Kane uses in her work at this point is a tape player for the music played to enhance relaxation and the Perkins Brailler on her desk. However, she plans to purchase a computer with speech or braille access in the next year to enable her to keep her own client mailing list and generate receipts and correspondence without the help of a sighted assistant.

Of the amount of business she gets, Kane says that one month may be extremely slow and the next brimming with new clients or old ones wanting to come in on a moment's notice. "If you are self-motivated, organized, and enjoy providing a sense of physical peace and well-being to others through touch," Susan Kane asserts, "I would recommend massage therapy as work that can be both psychologically and financially rewarding."

PAY AND BENEFITS: $45 per hour. Self-employment requires paying social security and employment taxes four times annually. Group rates for medical insurance are available through national organizations of massage therapists. Vacation for Kane comes "whenever I can afford to take it!"

MEDICAL TRANSCRIPTIONIST
Marion Fisher

"I supported a wife and four children with this work and never needed help from anyone. I'm very proud of that."

HOME
Bellflower, California

EMPLOYER
Kaiser Foundation Hospital

AGE
58

CAUSE OF BLINDNESS
Congenital glaucoma

VISUAL ACUITY
Totally blind since age three

N 1964, Marion Fisher supported his wife and three children on the unpredictable income he earned from work in commercial photo developing. But Missouri weather aggravated the children's frequent respiratory infections, Fisher was not finding much work, and his newly earned auto mechanic's license inspired fresh optimism. The family packed up their Missouri memories and headed for the West Coast.

Looking back, Fisher says he probably would not be so bold today, but the risk proved lucky enough for him. His U.S. Trade School diploma in auto mechanics and diesel fuel injection never did land him a job in southern California, but after a stint with door-to-door sales, he heard that Los Angeles County was hiring typists. He decided to take the test. It had been 12 years, he recalls, since his 1953 graduation from the Missouri School for the Blind, where he had excelled in typing classes for three consecutive years—and his speed was still good enough to get him on the county payroll as a transcriber-typist.

Eventually, Fisher enrolled in a nine-week medical transcribing class, then a one-semester medical secretary course. With his additional skills, he qualified for a job as medical transcriptionist at Rancho Los Amigos Hospital in Los Angeles County. The work suited him. He has been doing it for over 20 years, the last 15 of them with Kaiser Foundation Hospital in Bellflower, California.

The job of medical transcriptionist is one that requires concentration, accuracy, and speed. There are more than 900 doctors' names listed in a special file Fisher has assembled in his Braille 'n Speak—a talking braille notebook—to which he refers routinely to verify the spellings of those names. A doctor can dictate a report from any Touch-tone phone in or outside of the hospital. Fisher and his co-workers then tap into that dictation from their consoles, listen carefully, and type exactly what they hear.

There are seven different types of reports, ranging from in-patient consultations to letters to discharge summaries. The average report is about two pages long, and Fisher transcribes 10 to 20 of them daily. Medical transcriptionists think of their work, however, more in terms of lines than pages. Eight hundred lines per day is the required quota for each transcriptionist, and Fisher can check his line count at the end of each report. He uses a talking calculator to add the lines as the evening wears on, to be sure that if he is falling short of the expected 800 lines he can crank his typing fingers into a higher gear. By choice, Fisher works the night shift, clocking into his cubicle at 4:30 every afternoon and starting the quiet walk home at 1:00 A.M.

At Kaiser, the system used for typing reports is a Wang 4230 word processor. "I'm rather proud of the fact," Fisher comments, "that the only assistance I've received from vocational rehabilitation was in the purchase of an Optacon with a CRT lens." It is with the Optacon, an electronic device that converts print images to tactile output, that he accesses information on the screen. To proofread, check his line count, or verify the last word typed, Fisher holds his Optacon lens to the screen. Although reading in this manner was revolutionary 15 years ago, Fisher recognizes that it is tedious at best today. For speed, efficiency, and relief from the arthritis that has developed in his right shoulder from holding the lens to the computer screen, his current hope is for a speech synthesizer and screen-access program.

Fisher has purchased a variety of adaptive technology devices himself and uses many of those devices on the job. His Braille 'n Speak contains a number of words he frequently misspells and an ever-growing list of Latin and other medical terms; his talking calculator enables him to keep tabs on the number of lines typed daily; and his Franklin Language Master—a talking dictionary—has proved to be an outstanding addition to his work. Simple human interaction is always a valuable resource, too, Fisher says. "If I can't find a word, I can always ask a co-worker to look it up for me. In the same way, someone will often ask me to come listen to a bit of dictation that just makes no sense!"

Skills needed for the job beyond typing and a knowledge of spelling include the ability to listen, understand, and retain information. It is important to be able to anticipate phrases at times, too, and to have a mind that is receptive to new information. There are new drugs, new instruments, and new procedures mentioned all the time, and an integral part of Fisher's job is learning to recognize and spell them.

As for disadvantages, Fisher says a job with a little more physical movement might be nice. In addition, there is just the pitfall of suggestibility. "I can wind up with every ache and pain under the sun listening to those reports," he chuckles. "You can type a patient summary and say to yourself, 'Oh, yeah, I hurt there and I hurt there and I hurt there, too!'"

On a more serious note, however, Marion Fisher believes that medical transcribing is a good job for a person who is blind. The pay is good, his benefits are outstanding, and the work continues to be interesting. "I supported a wife and four children with this work and never needed help from anyone," Fisher says. I'm very proud of that."

PAY AND BENEFITS: $17.50 per hour; at Fisher's job, the top of the scale generally is reached after four years. Complete medical benefits, including coverage for all prescriptions and doctor visits; retirement plan; life insurance; and four weeks of paid vacation.

PIANO TUNER-TECHNICIAN
Pat Votta

"With the same customers calling me back after 20 years, I guess I must be a pretty good and experienced tuner-technician."

HOME
Brooklyn, New York

EMPLOYER
Self-employed

AGE
49

CAUSE OF BLINDNESS
Congenital glaucoma

VISUAL ACUITY
No vision

"**I**N TERMS of my education and focusing in on what to do with my life, losing my sight was one of the best things that ever happened to me," comments Pat Votta. Adding that most sighted people would never understand what he means by such a statement, Pat Votta tells the tale so familiar to young people with visual impairments. At 49, he recalls a public school situation where "sight conservation" was the label for classrooms that claimed him, and the expectation was always that he would use whatever vision he had to read print. Soon after his 16th birthday, he quit New York City's Lafayette High School and did not realize until age 22, after losing the remainder of his sight and studying braille, that he was not stupid, after all.

He learned braille easily, Votta recalls, but the essence of the lesson was not in the characters themselves but in the realization that "I really could learn." At the New York Association for the Blind (The Lighthouse), along with the usual rehabilitation complement of learning to "cook some food and wash my face and have mobility with a white cane," Votta also studied for and eventually acquired his general equivalency diploma. A prevocational evaluation directed Votta toward the agency's two-year course in piano tuning and, ultimately, to a 20-plus-year career.

For his first few years, Votta worked mostly as an independent contractor for Baldwin Piano Company, sometimes traveling great distances "just to get the work." Eventually, however, he built his own clientele and has operated entirely independently for years. A mix of private homes, piano teachers, and businesses, Votta's customers now number about 200. "I have about five recording studios who are regular customers," Votta explains, "and they account for quite a bit of my business. One recording studio might have you come back two or three times a week, or they might even pay you just to be there while a professional singer is making an album—just in case the piano goes out of tune." He travels to each customer on his own, using New

York's subways and buses and his own fondness for walking as transportation.

Votta loves his job and loves being in business for himself. He believes that a city like New York is the easiest place for a blind person to manage as he has. Although some piano technicians work for a particular company—tuning pianos at the same site day after day—Votta believes he can be more financially successful by going where his customers need him. He also enjoys the other benefits of working on his own. "I get to see different instruments all the time," he says with an almost infectious enthusiasm. "I get to meet new people every day—and I'm always out. I just love being outside."

Taking two to four subways a day is no hardship for Votta, and carrying 16 pounds of piano tools everywhere he goes is just business as usual, too. Like any piano tuner, he totes a case loaded with a tuning hammer and tuning fork, mutes, wire cutters, pliers, glue, and other tools. Attached to his tool case Votta also carries a leather pouch with additional piano parts, braille writing equipment, and a spare cane (having lost a few off subway platforms and to moving automobiles).

And what about customers' reactions to his blindness? "I always tell new people on the phone that I'm blind," Votta says, "and occasionally, there's someone who can't deal with it. If they can't, I don't go." Most people, however, make no comment about blindness. In fact, when going to a private residence, Votta will frequently call from the train station to ask the customer to watch for him in the next half hour lest he miss the house, and some are so nonchalant about his blindness, they have forgotten to look out the window!

Pat Votta still uses the braille he learned over 20 years ago to keep track of his customers and the dates when their most recent tunings were done. Three years ago, he added a laptop computer to his arsenal of tools for an organized professional. With his computer, he prints out all invoices, letters, and envelopes for his customers himself. His mailing list is also on the computer, and when he sends out his monthly reminder cards to those customers whose pianos are due for a visit, he uses the computer and laser printer to address the envelopes.

Before leaving each morning, Votta routinely leaves a voice memo on his answering machine tape to let his wife know where he will be for the day. He carries a microcassette recorder in his pocket at all times for quick notes. "If I'd known that piano tuning was some kind of blind stereotype," Votta says reflectively, "I probably never would have gone into it." He did not know, and he did get into it, and he has never had regrets. Over the years, he has met former teachers, counselors, and accountants who have changed careers to become piano technicians. Many have unimpaired sight and master's degrees, he says, but they are not any better at doing the job.

"There's an old saying you have to tune a thousand pianos before you're a good tuner," he laughs.

"That just means you need experience. With the same customers calling me back after 20 years, I guess I must be a pretty good and experienced tuner-technician."

PAY AND BENEFITS: $45–60 per tuning; more for repairs or additional time. Votta is covered by his wife's medical insurance, but group rates are available through the Piano Technicians Guild. Has established own retirement plan.

PROSTHETICS PURCHASING AGENT
Peggy Shoel

"I became my own advocate."

<u>HOME</u>
Seattle, Washington

<u>EMPLOYER</u>
**Veterans Administration
Medical Center**

<u>AGE</u>
59

<u>CAUSE OF BLINDNESS</u>
Diabetic retinopathy

<u>VISUAL ACUITY</u>
20/400

LIKE MILLIONS of women of her generation, Peggy Shoel's first full-time career was one without pay. She chauffeured her two sons everywhere from Scout meetings to sleep overs, volunteered for myriad community organizations, and served as president of the parent-teachers association. At age 45, she wanted a job and felt lucky to find one as a bookkeeper for the

Veterans Administration Medical Center just three miles from home.

After her first year of employment, however, her visual acuity abruptly plummeted from 20/20 to 20/400 as a result of diabetic retinopathy. In one traumatic 60-day period, she went from driving her own car to carrying a white cane, and a job change seemed in order. The result, Shoel says, is work that is perfect for her.

Peggy Shoel is one of four purchasing agents specifically charged with procuring prosthetics, orthotics, and sensory devices for veterans of the U.S. military. Her purchasing is an individualized affair, focusing one-on-one in each particular case. She purchases everything from leg braces and hearing aids to prosthetic limbs and talking computers, and each purchase order processed is for a veteran known to her as a human being.

Shoel consults with doctors, physical therapists, and social workers. She meets with patients and their caregivers, and she researches vendors, locates products, and directs the final purchase order to its proper destination. "You feel like you're doing something really good," explains an animated Shoel of her work. "I'm dealing with intelligent people all the time, and I'm always learning."

"You have to have good PR skills," Shoel continues, "because when people are hurting, they and their families can sometimes have short fuses." Shoel clearly possesses those necessary public relations skills. She also has a deep regard and sense of compassion for each veteran whose case is assigned to her. "We have a 27-year-old man going home soon," she cites as an example, "who has a high spinal cord injury and can't breathe on his own. He needs a ventilator, aspirator, special bed, and commode, and we need to make certain all that equipment is ready for him when he gets home, so he won't be medically compromised."

Of the $2 million worth of equipment her department bought last year, Shoel says the most common items are custom wheelchairs. In addition to purchasing prosthetics, each agent makes purchases in his or her area of specialization. Shoel's area includes beds, patient lifts, and adaptive equipment for people who are blind.

Requests come in for closed-circuit televisions, magnifiers, talking watches, reading machines, electric razors, and tape recorders, and a team that includes an optometrist, a physician, a social worker, and Shoel reviews each one separately. Having to keep abreast of the vendors of access technology and related products for visually impaired people has enabled Shoel, the medical center's only blind employee, to improve her own job effectiveness, too.

Since first losing her sight, Shoel has depended heavily on a closed-circuit television, magnifiers, and a large talking calculator as equipment to do her job. Two years ago, however, she realized that she was falling increasingly behind the pace of her co-workers because the computerization that was enhancing their efficiency was inaccessible to her.

"I became my own advocate," Shoel recalls proudly. There was resistance at first, and her employer wanted some evidence that she could use a computer before money was spent on adaptive equipment. Ultimately, however, she won her tool of equality—a large-print computer monitor, which gave her access to the same software her co-workers were using. "I was terrified," she remembers with amusement. "I was certain I'd push a button that would make a light go off in our director's office to announce I'd ruined the whole system!"

Today her fears are an entertaining memory, as Shoel confidently cuts purchase orders and processes other information with the aid of her enlarged computer screen and closed-circuit television. Her technology, she says, has enabled her to do all the same tasks as her co-workers—and her delight in doing them is unmistakable.

In regard to acceptance of blindness, Shoel says of her workplace, "It's an absolutely wonderful place to work. Everyone is so supportive and encouraging." There is another bonus, she points out, for someone who, after transporting others around for over 20 years, now finds her own transportation a daily challenge: The medical center has an abundance of other services all under one roof. If Shoel has prescriptions to fill, gifts to buy, dry cleaning to drop off, or a watch to repair, it can all be done before or after work in the very same building. After 14 years on this government job,

Shoel has yet to find any significant drawbacks. "I love it," she summarizes with a satisfied smile, "I just absolutely love it."

PAY AND BENEFITS: About $25,000 annually. Wide selection of medical packages; about 26 vacation days annually after 15 years.

RECEPTIONIST
Barbara Browning

"Reception work is very accessible to blind people, but it's essential to be aware of your surroundings and always to know who's coming in and going out."

HOME
San Rafael, California

EMPLOYER
Guide Dogs for the Blind

AGE
48

CAUSE OF BLINDNESS
Congenital glaucoma

VISUAL ACUITY
No vision

"S OMETIMES you call a place," comments Barbara Browning, "and the receptionist sounds as though she's doing you a big favor by answering the phone. At a place like this, it's especially important that people hear a friendly voice."

A "place like this" is Guide Dogs for the Blind in San Rafael, California, where Browning has worked as receptionist for 12 years. Calling her answering style "friendly" is an understatement! Her signature warmth and sunny disposition are immediately apparent to first-time callers and familiar friends alike.

Browning's coming to her job represents a type of fantasy that many have entertained but few have pursued. As a student of Guide Dogs in 1972, Browning fell in love with the place and remembers thinking "I'd love to work here." She carried that yen back home to Los Angeles with her, where she was working as a braille proofreader of English, German, and Spanish texts. Finally in 1981, after training with another dog from the school, she acted. As serendipity will sometimes have it, Browning's letter arrived at Guide Dogs simultaneously with the impending retirement of the school's receptionist. The rest, as they say, is history.

There had never been a receptionist—or any other staff member—at the school who was blind, and Browning has never taken the responsibility of that "firstness" lightly. She has purchased assorted pieces of adaptive equipment over the years to enable her to function more independently on the job and has looked for new duties to add to her workload.

Her first task in the morning is to check for messages with the school's answering service and convey those immediately to their recipients. She types them quickly and quietly (as she does all other messages throughout the day) into her BrailleMate, a talking braille notebook, which she purchased to replace a VersaBraille II two years ago. The telephone extensions of all 110 Guide Dogs employees are also contained in the BrailleMate, as is other useful information.

On her neatly organized desk, Browning keeps file boxes of brailled information that is frequently useful to callers. On one morning, for example, she gives three different callers who want pets the names and telephone numbers of other possible sources. "Our waiting list is two years long," she explains, "but you might try Pets in Need or Labrador Rescue."

Some want to give dogs to the school, and Browning is often able to save everyone time and energy with just a few initial questions. Still others want information about the school's graduation ceremonies (always open to the public), ask about tours for interested scout or school groups, or have an interest in volunteering. Browning has a flattering measure of sweetness, enthusiasm, and information for them all, managing always to answer several more calls, take quick messages, and, if necessary, deal with visitors or deliveries that arrive.

"Reception work is very accessible to blind people," Browning believes, "but it's essential to be aware of your surroundings and always to know who's coming in and going out." She greets each person who enters and admits that good voice recognition on her part helps. Knowing the layout of the building in which she works is also essential, since she frequently escorts visitors to appropriate offices.

Beyond taking calls, relaying messages, and occasionally typing letters (for which she uses an Optacon lens—an electronic device that converts screen images to a tactile array—to check for errors), Browning assumes another large and ongoing responsibility: education. For many who enter the dog guide school, Browning represents a first encounter with a blind person. It is important to her that the encounter be remembered as a positive one.

She takes time, she says, to demonstrate the braillewriter, Optacon, or BrailleMate because it makes others feel comfortable with her blindness. Browning fields questions, she says, ranging from "the mushy-gushy ones who think it's wonderful that you get out of bed in the morning to the ones who simply want to know about modifications you make to get your job done." All of it is important, particularly in an environment where blindness is center stage.

For graduates of the school, Browning's presence has another plus. When they call with the pain of impending dog retirement or other canine-related dilemmas, the first person to take the call is herself an empathetic dog guide user. "I can't give advice about training," she says, "because I'm just a dog user myself, not a trainer. But I can listen, and maybe I cheer people up a little because I understand."

Indeed, this receptionist's welcome to callers is as sunny as California itself and, in keeping with that demeanor, the sometimes sleeping, sometimes tail-wagging dog guide at her feet is named—what else?—Sunshine.

PAY AND BENEFITS: About $24,000 annually. Good medical and dental coverage; life insurance; and, after 12 years, four weeks of vacation.

REFRIGERATION MECHANIC
Tim Schneebeck

"I wanted to work with my hands, not with my head."

HOME
Seattle, Washington

EMPLOYER
Self-employed, T&M Refrigeration

AGE
43

CAUSE OF BLINDNESS
Retinopathy of prematurity

VISUAL ACUITY
"I used to have light perception, but in 1972, I fell off an extension ladder and put my lights out!"

"TIM, WE'VE got a furnace problem in Building 564," says the voice on Tim Schneebeck's answering machine, heard via remote on the cellular telephone Schneebeck carries in his car. "Call me at Fort Lawton and I'll give you the details." Schneebeck zips through a few more messages about failing ice machines and refrigeration units, while writing phone numbers in his Braille 'n Speak—a talking braille notebook—punching a call into the cellular phone, and making a comment to Willie, his driver.

Another message heard on the telephone's speaker explains, "I got your name from someone who said you could work on this heat pump I have; it's made by the Conserve Corporation." Schneebeck groans in recognition of the product, as Willie finds a parking place at the curb of a teen club in Seattle's university district. "We'll need the CO_2 tank here and the socket set," Schneebeck instructs, as he climbs out of the Chevy Celebrity station wagon that serves as vehicle, office, and toolshed for his business.

"It's not a clean-hands job," Schneebeck will tell you bluntly of his now-15 years in business for himself as T&M Refrigeration. Technically, he is a refrigeration mechanic and certified boiler repairperson. In reality, he maintains and repairs everything from commercial refrigeration and air conditioning units to oil furnaces, swimming pools, and dishwashers. His work takes him into such humble settings as dugout crawl spaces, weather-worn rooftops, sooty furnace rooms, and greasy kitchens—and he thrives on it.

Approximately 100 customers keep him busy five days a week year-round, with business fluctuating unpredictably from one season to another. Larger accounts—like the Army Reserve Center's 30 buildings from Bellingham to Tumwater and the 100-room Landmark Hotel, where Schneebeck is responsible for maintenance of everything from the air conditioning and heating to laundry equipment and dishwashers—keep his income relatively stable.

Overhead is fairly low. Schneebeck does all the work himself, with minor assistance from Willie. When cleaning the coils on a nightclub's ice machine, for instance, he asks Willie to describe the dust cloud created by the carbon dioxide just released. Repairing a restaurant's refrigeration unit, he calls upon Willie to read temperatures and pressure gauges as he increases the level of refrigerant. And when cleaning the scanner on an oil burner, he is informed by Willie when the glass is clear.

Most of the work, however, is done by sound and touch. Schneebeck's ear is as tuned to the noise of motors as a trained musician's is to pitch, and his hands are as familiar with the components in a commercial clothes dryer as an architect's eye is with a blueprint. The only tool or technique he avoids, he says, is an acetylene torch. Soldering is a requirement of anyone working as his driver-assistant because, as Schneebeck quips, "I'm rather attached to my hands."

For Tim Schneebeck, the educational process for the work he does today stretches back to childhood. When he was in public elementary school in Tacoma, Washington, he remembers the school custodian as one of his favorite people, the boiler room as a lunchtime haven. "There were so many machinists in my family," he laughs, "that repairing and running machines was probably in my blood." His maternal grandfather ran a machine shop in Colorado Springs, and childhood summers were spent visiting Granddad and learning what he knew. "He never taught me how to turn a machine on," Schneebeck recalls, "before first teaching me how to turn it off. The lesson has served me well."

Schneebeck's proudest memories from high school center around such occasions as restoring pinball machines and repairing the school's public address system. Recalling a visit to a neighbor's photo studio, he recounts asking if he could investigate why the room was so uncomfortably warm. "He was one of the many people who believed in me," Schneebeck recalls, "so I charged the unit with more refrigerant, and it ran smoothly for another 20 years." Growing up with people who believed in his ability until he demonstrated otherwise, Schneebeck contends, was the most significant factor in his preparation for his success today. He indicates that the "system" (rehabilitation services for people who are blind) was far less supportive of a job choice that seemed unusual.

Although he never completed a degree, Schneebeck spent the better part of six years in and out of college programs in mechanical engineering and computer programming. "The state [rehabilitation services] was happy to support my doing any of those things," he says, "but they just couldn't accept that I wanted to work with my hands, not with my head."

In 1978, Schneebeck went into business for himself and has never looked back with regret. His adaptive equipment is minimal: a volt meter with speech output, a Braille 'n Speak, and soon a desktop computer with speech output. Other electronic equipment relevant to his efficiency on the job includes his pager, cellular telephone, and telephone answering machine, and an electronic device for locking and unlocking his car.

The first few hours each morning are spent ordering parts and scheduling. The station wagon is always stocked with basics—a ladder on top, and the back piled high with air filters, refrigerant, oil burner service tools, screwdrivers, socket sets, and an assortment of spare parts. Schneebeck likes to keep things as simple as possible, depending most heavily on his hands and vast mechanical know-how to get jobs done.

With his Braille 'n Speak and a printer, he prepares all invoices himself, as well as keeps records of accounts, service contracts, part numbers, and more. His $45-an-hour rate is standard in the refrigeration business, he says, but what may not be is his policy of giving free estimates and the philosophy that "if I don't fix it, you don't pay."

The philosophy has served him well. His days are as full as his answering machine, and his customers, from hotel managers to restaurant owners, are visibly glad to see him show up. Occasionally, Schneebeck says, a new customer will show bewilderment at his blindness, but "when I go to work and fix the problem, they stop worrying about it."

A yellow pages ad and word of mouth are Schneebeck's primary advertising tools, and they seem to be sufficient. As one club proprietor puts it: "The guy just really knows his stuff."

PAY AND BENEFITS: About $1,700 a month, after paying for medical and life insurance. Time off is sparse; Schneebeck attends a three-day annual convention each summer, makes one trip to the beach, and always shuts down to attend the local hydroplane race.

SMALL-ENGINE MECHANIC
Gary Petsch

"The only difference between a blind mechanic and a sighted one is that the blind one is better organized."

HOME
Hopkinsville, Kentucky

EMPLOYER
U.S. Army Facility of Engineers

AGE
43

CAUSE OF BLINDNESS
Diabetic retinopathy

VISUAL ACUITY
No vision

HE ONLY difference between a blind mechanic and a sighted one," affirms Gary Petsch, "is that the blind one is better organized." He should know. He has been troubleshooting, rebuilding, and overhauling engines for the U.S. Army for 10 years. At Fort Campbell, an army post straddling the Tennessee-Kentucky border, Petsch works as a small-engine mechanic for the army's Facility of Engineers.

Technically, a small engine is any under 20 horsepower, and in Petsch's job these engines might come in the form of chain saws, jaws of life, mobile generators, or any other machinery used on the 35,000-employee base. Each of the three mechanics in the garage has a specialty, and Petsch's is engines of weed eaters and push mowers. Although on and off the job he has actually worked on engines of all types and sizes—from automobiles to tractors—he admits that the small engine has some advantages for a mechanic who is blind: "Everything," he says, "fits on one bench."

Petsch does whatever any sighted mechanic would do, with the addition of a few adaptive tools and techniques. "I always take an engine apart by sections," he explains. "When the muffler comes off, all the bolts stay with that muffler." And thus he works section by section, on the carburetor, intake manifold, and other components, putting each piece of the component where he can locate and identify it later.

While the army may have been reluctant to hire him in the first place, experience has removed all doubt. The first day, Petsch recalls, "They would have been satisfied if I'd fixed just one engine—and I fixed 20."

Ordinarily, the average number of engines Petsch works on per day is about 15, and he has proven himself many times over to his employer in other ways as well. Named Handicapped Employee of the Year at Fort Campbell twice, Petsch has also tasted the thrill of being National Handicapped Employee of the Year in 1987, a distinction that earned him a week at the Pentagon. He is known throughout his Hopkinsville, Kentucky, community as a Sunday school teacher, Scoutmaster, golfer, and runner.

When Petsch lost his sight at age 31 as a result of diabetic retinopathy, he immediately began looking at ideas for a career change. Building other people's houses had been his work, and although he now believes that a blind person can do everything essential to carpentry, he did not want a job where someone else had to take him to a different site each day. His vocational rehabilitation counselor, as Petsch puts it, "wanted to send me to college because they think a blind person can't do anything else." After a year and a half of earning mostly *A*'s at Brigham Young University, however, Petsch knew he was in the wrong place. He wanted to go back to working with his hands.

Queries eventually led him to a new program at Arkansas Enterprises for the Blind, where he enrolled and found himself to be the only student with no usable vision. It did not worry him. He never doubted, he says, that there was nothing he could not do if he had the will and determination.

Petsch uses the standard toolbox issued to every army mechanic and makes only minor adaptations. He developed a timing method while in the

Arkansas training program, which is now used by other mechanics who are blind. "Everything in an engine has to open and close at the same time, or you don't pop in the gas when you need it," Petsch explains in his casual, confident manner. "It used to be that a blind person needed help timing an engine, because there's a little timing mark on the cam gear that you need to see. I developed a method where a blind person could use a ruler, find a different reference point, and do it without sight. If you're trying to get a job, and you say 'Well, you'll have to help me do this and help me do that,' it isn't going to help you any. The more independent you can be, the better your chance of getting a job."

Petsch has a 20-foot ruler with braille markings every six inches that is attached to a six-inch ruler with braille indications at one-eighth-inch increments. He also has a braille square. His most recent acquisitions, braille micrometers and a braille multimeter, have increased his independence even further, enabling him to check ohm, volt, and amp counts without sight. His most sophisticated adaptive technology devices, he says, are his talking blood pressure and glucose monitors at home.

Also at home are a radial arm saw and full complement of tools, which, as is the case with his mechanic's tools, Petsch believes he uses far more safely without his sight than he ever did with. In his after-work hours, he has already helped a friend build a home addition and is currently building himself a garage. As far as people accepting his blindness at work, he answers emphatically, "Now they do."

PAY AND BENEFITS: About $26,000 a year, at the top of the range. Good medical coverage, life insurance, retirement plan. After ten years, four weeks of paid vacation.

Resources

Resources

A WIDE VARIETY of organizations and companies disseminate information, distribute adaptive equipment, and provide various forms of assistance to people who are blind or visually impaired, their families, and the professionals who work with them. This section contains a sample listing of these organizations and companies. Additional information can be found in the *Directory of Services for Blind and Visually Impaired Persons in the United States and Canada, 24th Edition*, published by the American Foundation for the Blind.

Sources of Information

American Council of the Blind
1155 15th Street, N.W., Suite 720
Washington, DC 20005
(202) 467-5081 or (800) 424-8666
The American Council of the Blind (ACB) is a consumer organization that promotes effective participation of blind people in all aspects of society. It provides information and referral, legal assistance, scholarships, advocacy, consultation services, and program development assistance and publishes *The Braille Forum.*

American Foundation for the Blind

15 West 16th Street
New York, NY 10011
(212) 620-2000 or (800) 232-5463

The American Foundation for the Blind (AFB) provides a wide variety of services to and acts as an information clearinghouse for people who are blind or visually impaired and their families, professionals, organizations, schools, and corporations. It conducts information and educational programs; provides consultative services; stimulates research to improve services to visually impaired persons; sells adaptive products; advocates for services and legislation; produces videos; and publishes books, pamphlets, the *Directory of Services for Blind and Visually Impaired Persons in the United States and Canada,* and the *Journal of Visual Impairment & Blindness.* AFB maintains the following regional centers across the country, as well as a governmental relations department in Washington, DC.:

AFB Resource Center

100 Peachtree Street, Suite 620
Atlanta, GA 30303
(404) 525-2303
Serves Georgia, Puerto Rico, and the Virgin Islands.

Eastern Regional Center

1615 M Street, N.W., Suite 250

Washington, DC 20036
(202) 457-1487
Serves Connecticut, Delaware, District of Columbia, Maine, Maryland, Massachusetts, New Hampshire, New Jersey, New York, North Carolina, Pennsylvania, Rhode Island, South Carolina, Vermont, and Virginia.

Midwest Regional Center
401 North Michigan Avenue, Suite 308
Chicago, IL 60611
(312) 245-9961
Serves Illinois, Indiana, Iowa, Kentucky, Michigan, Minnesota, Missouri, North Dakota, Ohio, South Dakota, Tennessee, West Virginia, and Wisconsin.

Southwest Regional Center
260 Treadway Plaza
Exchange Park
Dallas, TX 75235
(214) 352-7222
Serves Alabama, Arkansas, Colorado, Florida, Kansas, Louisiana, Mississippi, Montana, Nebraska, New Mexico, Oklahoma, Texas, and Wyoming.

Western Regional Center
111 Pine Street, Suite 725
San Francisco, CA 94111
(415) 392-4845
Serves Alaska, Arizona, California, Guam, Hawaii, Idaho, Nevada, Oregon, Utah, and Washington.

Association for Education and Rehabilitation of the Blind and Visually Impaired (AER)

206 North Washington Street, Suite 320
Alexandria, VA 22314
(703) 548-1884

The Association for Education and Rehabilitation of the Blind and Visually Impaired (AER) is a professional membership organization that promotes all phases of education for and work with blind and visually impaired persons of all ages, strives to expand their opportunities to take a contributory place in society, and disseminates information. It also certifies rehabilitation teachers, orientation and mobility specialists, and classroom teachers and publishes *RE:view, AER Report,* and *Job Exchange Monthly.*

Canadian National Institute for the Blind

1931 Bayview Avenue
Toronto, Ontario M4G 4C8
Canada
(416) 480-7580

The Canadian National Institute for the Blind (CNIB) provides an array of services to blind and visually impaired persons, including orientation and mobility training and rehabilitation teaching.

National Federation of the Blind

1800 Johnson Street
Baltimore, MD 21230
(410) 659-9314

The National Federation of the Blind (NFB) is a consumer organization that strives to improve social and economic conditions of blind persons, evaluates and assists in establishing programs, and provides public education and scholarships. It also publishes *The Braille Monitor* and *Future Reflections*.

Sources of Products

Blazie Engineering
105 East Jarrettsville Road
Forest Hill, MD 21050
(410) 893-9333
Blazie Engineering manufactures Braille 'n Speak and Type 'n Speak, portable notetakers and information managers that offer braille keyboards and speech output.

Franklin Electronic Publishers
122 Burrs Road
Mount Holly, NJ 08060
(800) 762-5382
Franklin Electronic Publishers distributes the Franklin Language Master, a hand-held talking dictionary with a typewriter keyboard that includes features such as a thesaurus, spelling corrector, and grammar guide.

Henter-Joyce
10901-C Roosevelt Boulevard, Suite 1200
St. Petersburg, FL 33716
(813) 576-5658 or (800) 336-5658

Henter-Joyce distributes JAWS (Job Access With Speech), a screen-access software program to be used with a speech synthesizer.

HumanWare
6245 King Road
Loomis, CA 95650
(916) 652-7253
HumanWare distributes KeyNote Gold, an internal or external speech synthesizer that is also available in a credit-card-size format; KeyNote Companion, a palmtop computer with speech synthesis; KeyBraille and Alva refreshable braille displays; and Romeo braille embossers.

TeleSensory
455 North Bernardo Avenue
P.O. Box 7455
Mountain View, CA 94039-7455
(415) 960-0920
TeleSensory distributes OPTACON II, a device that converts printed characters to a vibrating tactile array; BrailleMate, a portable computer device for word processing and record management that offers speech output, a braille keyboard, and a single-cell braille display; and a full complement of access-technology products, including refreshable braille displays, braille embossers, screen-magnification software and hardware, products that provide access to synthesized speech, and optical character recognition equipment.

IN ADDITION, several publications contain assessments of and information about assistive technology, including the following periodicals:

Journal of Visual Impairment & Blindness
American Foundation for the Blind
15 West 16th Street
New York, NY 10011
(212) 620-2148
The *Journal of Visual Impairment & Blindness* is the monthly international journal of record on blindness and visual impairment. Its "Random Access" column features announcements and evaluations of new adaptive technology devices and programs.

TACTIC Magazine
Clovernook Printing House for the Blind
7000 Hamilton Avenue
Cincinnati, OH 45231
(513) 522-3860
TACTIC Magazine is a quarterly on assistive technology, covering hardware and software that enables computer access through braille, synthesized speech, or enlarged print.

About the Author

Deborah Kendrick is an award-winning writer, editor, columnist, and poet. The writer of the column "Alive and Well" for the *Cincinnati Enquirer,* she is also editor of *Tactic,* a quarterly that focuses on access technology, and writes on family issues as contributing editor for *Dialogue,* a general-interest magazine for blind people. She has written hundreds of articles, many of them on disability-related issues, for the *Cincinnati Enquirer, Woman's Day, Parenting,* and many other publications and is a frequent speaker on topics related to disability awareness. Named a "role model for women" by Women in Communications, Inc. and recipient of the American Foundation for the Blind's 1993 Access Award, she has received numerous other honors for her efforts as both journalist and advocate, including the 1992 Young Alumni Achievement Award from Adrian College and the National Easter Seal Society's 1990 EDI Journalism Award. Blind since early childhood and a former teacher of visually impaired children and adults, she has three children and lives in Cincinnati, Ohio.

THE MISSION of the American Foundation for the Blind (AFB) is to enable persons who are blind or visually impaired to achieve equality of access and opportunity that will ensure freedom of choice in their lives.

It is the policy of the American Foundation for the Blind to use in the first printing of its books acid-free paper that meets the ANSI Z39.48 Standard. The infinity symbol that appears above indicates that the paper in this printing meets that standard.